tropical fish

guide to selection,
care and compatibility

Written by
Lance Jepson MA VetMB CBiol MSB MRCVS

tropical· fish

guide to selection,
care and compatibility

Written by
Lance Jepson MA VetMB CBiol MSB MRCVS

Magnet & Steel Ltd

www.magnetsteel.com

Printed and bound in South Korea.

ISBN: 978-1-907337-19-2
ISBN: 1-907337-19-9

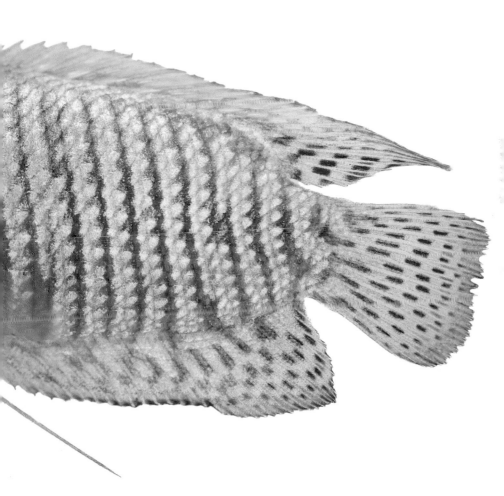

Contents

Tropical fish

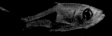

you consider the range of different selectively-bred varieties of the commoner species.

World-wide the tropical fish hobby is a multi-million pound industry, with the vast majority of ornamental freshwater fish captive bred on commercial fish farms, and a small number produced locally by hobbyists. One of the major expenses with keeping tropical fish is maintaining a high enough temperature, typically around 25°C (77°F). It is therefore no surprise that most of these fish farms are found in tropical or warm temperate places such as Singapore, Malaysia, southern China, Florida and Hawaii, where temperatures allow the outdoor culture of the majority of fish. However some unexpected countries also have a small presence, such as Czechoslovakia and Israel.

The rest of the fish available are wild caught. Here improved transportation techniques, faster and more reliable air travel and inroads into previously inaccessible areas and countries such as Myanmar (Burma) has dramatically increased the range of species available.

This is not without consequence however. In recent years certain popular fish with small natural ranges have been over collected for the aquarium trade with serious declines in their wild populations – this has occurred with both the Galaxy Danio (Danio margaritatus) in Myanmar, and Denison's barb (Puntius denisonii) from India. The Red-Tailed Black Shark (Epalzeorhynchus bicolor) is believed to be extinct in the wild. Fortunately all of these species are being captive bred in their thousands.

Most of the ornamental fish commonly available are tropical fish that are likely to need supplementary heating and in the species discussions, tropical represents a temperature range of 22 to 26°C (72 to 79F) unless otherwise stated. However, some fish do prefer it cooler and are happy at normal, ambient room temperatures. Such fish are called temperate and this represents a range of 18 to 22°C (64 to 72F), although a few degrees either side can be tolerated. Some fish are naturally subject to wide seasonal variations and can be kept in either tropical or temperate aquaria.

Those fish described as omnivores are generalist feeders that will eat a variety of flake, pelleted and frozen foods.

Selection

The successful setting up of an aquarium is covered in the companion volume to this, *Aquarium*. This book is to help choose from the many different fish and invertebrates commonly available in aquatics outlets to start you on your fish-keeping hobby.

When making your choices please take into account the final size of the fish, and its compatibility – both with other members of the same species (does it live as a shoal or is it territorial?) and with other types of fish. These all affect how many of the fish you can have in total. More detailed advice on stocking densities is given in *Aquarium*.

General guidelines for choosing your fish are:

- Less is more. Shoaling fish always look better in larger numbers of the same species.

- Rule of Odds. Where possible buy odd numbers of shoaling fish, as this looks more natural.

- Do not buy fish solely as janitors. See the sections on Catfish for further explanation.

- Dither fish are mentioned in several places. Dither fish are smaller, active shoaling fish that impart a sense of security to the rest of the aquarium inhabitants.

- Only select from healthy fish. Look at the other fish in the same tank. If there are any obviously sick ones, or worse still dead fish, then do not buy any from that tank. Many fish diseases are very infectious in the confines of an aquarium, so even if the fish you want looks well, there is a high chance that it will be incubating the same problem.

Bringing your fish home

Your fish will be placed into a plastic bag by the shop for transportation home. Place it into a dark bag or carrier to reduce stress. If possible use an insulated carrier (as marketed for frozen goods) to reduce heat loss during the journey home.

Once home:

1. Switch off the aquarium lights.

2. Float the bag in your aquarium for around 15 to 20 minutes to allow the temperatures of the bag and the aquarium to equalise.

3. Open or cut into the bag and start to introduce small amounts of aquarium water into the bag a little and often, so that the fish will gradually become used to the water in the aquarium. This should take 20 to 30 minutes.

4. Once acclimatised, gently tip the bag to allow your new fish to swim out into its new home.

Alternatively, and this applies particularly if the fish has badly fouled its transport water, do the first two stages, but then siphon some water from your aquarium into a suitable bucket or container and release the fish into this water. Then net the fish out and place it into your aquarium.

Types of fish

Barbs

Barbs are small to medium-sized cyprinids that are ideal community fish for those aquaria housing larger or more robust fish, such as cichlids. Typically they are social fish that form loose schools, a behaviour they will exhibit if housed In a large enough aquarium. The nomenclature of these small cyprinids is in some confusion and in many books these fish are assigned to the genus Barbus, rather than Puntius used here.

Rosy Barb
Puntius conchonius

Origin: Northern India, Assam and Bengal
Length: 10 to 15 cm (4 to 6 in)
Lifespan: 5 years

In most varieties the males are a bright rose-red colour with variable black markings on the single fins. This may fade or intensify depending upon the reproductive readiness of the fish. In some varieties, especially the highly reflective metallic ones, this red colour has been lost. Adult males are larger but more slender than females.

Long-finned and highly metallic varieties are available. Occasionally individuals with large mirror-scales are seen. They are Omnivores. Can live in both tropical and temperate aquaria.

Good water quality is a must. Generally compatible with similarly sized or larger fish. It is an active shoaling fish so keep a minimum of three, preferably more. A scatter spawning egg-layer; will benefit from a cooler winter period (down to 15°C/59F). Wild rosy barbs are subjected to marked seasonal temperature variations, which is why they do well in both temperate and tropical aquaria.

Golden Barb
Puntius semifasciolatus

Origin: Southeast China including Hong Kong
Length: 7.5 to 10 cm (3 to 4 in)
Lifespan: 5 to 7 years

Males are smaller and more slender. This is a golden morph of the Green barb. Highly metallic and tricolour (piebald) varieties are also seen. They are omnivores. Will live in tropical and temperate. Good water quality essential. Good with similar-sized or large fish. Sociable, so keep 3 or more individuals. Egg scatterer. A hardy and peaceful barb, whose natural range gives it a wide temperature tolerance.

Tiger Barb
Puntius tetrazona

Origin: Indonesia including Sumatra and Borneo

Length: 5 to 7.5 cm (2 to 3 in)

Lifespan: 6 years

Males are smaller, thinner and the colours, especially the red on the fins, are brighter. Many varieties exist, including green/moss (the black bars are extended and merge together), albino, platinum (highly metallic) and harlequin are available. Omnivore. Tropical. Prefers softer, more acidic water (pH 6.5) but modern varieties are happy in a wide range of waters. Susceptible to high nitrite levels. Generally fine with similar-sized or larger fish. Single fish and the odd individual likely to fin-nip, so they should be kept in small schools of at least five fish, which are then more likely to concentrate on each other and ignore tank-mates. Egg scatterers. An ideal fish for a species-only planted aquarium where a large shoal of a single variety would form a dramatic display. Avoid keeping with smaller, slow-moving or long-finned fish such as guppies or Siamese fighting fish.

Similar species

Odessa Barb
Puntius padamya

Origin: Central Myanmar
Length: 6 cm (2.5 in)
Lifespan: 3 to 5 years

Adult males will show an intense red band along the
mid-line. For a long time this fish was a conundrum
and was thought to be a cultured variety, or possibly
a hybrid, produced in Russia – hence the name
"Odessa". In 2008 it was "discovered" and described
in its native Myanmar. Occasionally marketed as
Ticto barbs, which is a distinct species
P. ticto ticto. Tropical or temperate.

Cherry Barb
Puntius titteya

Origin: Sri Lanka
Length: A small barb up to 5 cm (2 in)
Lifespan 5 to 7 years

The Males are slimmer and redder, the colouring becoming more intense during breeding.
Cherry barbs are commercially captive-bred in their thousands, which is a good thing. The IUCN list the Cherry Barb as Conservation Dependant because of heavy collection in the wild, so avoid wild-caught specimens. Albino and long-finned varieties are occasionally seen.

Red-Line/Torpedo/ Denison's Barb
Puntius denisonii

Origin: India
Length: 15 cm (6 in)
Lifespan: 5 to 8 years

Males are slimmer than females. Omnivore. Tropical and temperate. A riverine fish, so strong currents and aeration appreciated. Good with similar-sized or larger species. An active, sociable fish so keep at least three, preferably five or more. Egg layer. Bred commercially using hormonal injections. Denison's barbs are active fish that will require a large, preferably long, aquarium. Over collection for the aquarium trade and habitat degradation have lead to Denison's barb becoming listed by the IUCN as Vulnerable.

Danios

Danios are generally quite small cyprinids averaging around two to three cm body length (there are exceptions). They are peaceful, shoaling species that are tolerant of a wide range of water qualities, so much so that these can be the first additions to your aquarium when initiating biological cycling.

Zebra Danio

Danio rerio

Origin: India and Bangladesh
Length: 6 cm (2.4 in)
Lifespan: 5 years

Mature females are significantly plumper than the relatively slim male. In wild-type Zebra Danios the horizontal lines between dark stripes are yellow-gold in males and silvery in females. There is a naturally occurring spotted morph known as the Leopard danio (previously known as Brachydanio frankei). Common aquarium varieties are albino (gold) and long-finned, plus combinations of these. Omnivore. Tropical and temperate. Good water quality essential. An active shoaling fish best kept as a group of five or more. Egg scatterers that will eat their own eggs unless separated. These are the ultimate dither fish because their constant motion can give a sense of security to otherwise shy species – the danios' constant presence indicates that "all is well". The Zebra Danio has been used extensively in research and many laboratory strains have been developed. Genetically modified strains of Zebra danios containing fluorescent jellyfish proteins have been produced. The keeping of such genetically modified fish is illegal in the European Union, including the UK as well as Canada, Australia and Japan. In the USA they are banned in California.

Similar species

The **Pearl Danio** *Danio albolineatus* is slightly bigger, up to 8 cm, with a lifespan of up to five years and is suitable for both tropical and temperate aquaria.

The **Glowlight Danio** *Danio choprae* is smaller (up to 3 cm) with a vibrant mid-line bronze-coloured stripe and darker vertical striping. It can live up to three years and does best at tropical temperatures.

The **Giant Danio** *Devario aequipinnatus* grows significantly bigger than most other danios – to around 10 cm (4 in) and is suitable for tropical and temperate, providing the temperature does not dip below 18°C (64F). Lifespan five to seven years.

Galaxy or Celestial Pearl Danio
Danio margaritatus

Origin: Myanmar
Length: 21 mm (0.8 in)
Lifespan: 3 years, possibly up to 5

Males have brighter colours and a more defined pattern; females are slightly larger, with more rounded abdomens and paler colours. Omnivore. Tropical and temperate. Good water quality a must. Sociable; best kept in larger groups (10 or more) as males will spar, although damage beyond nipped fins is rare. They are so small that tank-mates may eat them; ideal for nano aquaria. Egg-layer. This tiny fish was only discovered in 2006 and became an immediate sensation. This led to rapid over collection in the wild such that the Myanmar Department of Fisheries banned their export. They are IUCN listed as Not Evaluated.

White Cloud Mountain Minnow
Tanichthys albonubes

Origin: China
Length: 4 cm (1.6 in)
Lifespan: 5 to 7 years

Males are slimmer and the red colouring of the single fins more pronounced. A gold form is frequently available and, occasionally, a long-finned variety. Omnivore. Tropical and temperate. Good water quality essential. A shoaling fish that does well in groups of five or more. An excellent species for the temperate nano-aquarium. Goldfish and other larger fish, may eat them. Egg layer. The bright metallic horizontal line from the nose to the tail is a brilliant blue in very young WCMMs. Although the WCMM is a staple of the hobby, and is easily bred, it is considered highly endangered and from 1980 to 2001 was thought to be extinct in the wild.

Harlequin Rasbora
Trigonostigma heteromorpha

Origin: South-east Asia
Length: 5 cm (2 in)
Lifespan: 6 years

Adult females are rounder and slightly larger than males. Normal, black, blue and golden forms. Micropredator, but will eat usual foods. Tropical. Avoid hard water, but otherwise good water quality is important. A very peaceful fish that does best as a shoal of 10 or more. This fish would make a stunning single species aquarium. Otherwise, keep with smaller, gentler species such as tetras. Egg-layer. Eggs are laid upsidedown on the underside of aquatic plant leaves. The Harlequin Rasbora is a justifiably long-standing favourite. Other similar-looking species are now regularly available such as **Espe's Rasbora** *T. espei* and **Hengel's Rasbora** *T. hengeli.*

Rosy Bitterling

Acheilognathus ocellatus ocellatus

Origin: Taiwan and China
Length: 7 cm (2.5 in)
Lifespan: 3 to 6 years

Males are brightly coloured when breeding; females have a black spot (ocellus) on the dorsal fin. Females ready to spawn develop an extremely long tube-like ovipositor for transferring their eggs into the host mussel. Omnivore. Temperate. Good water quality a must. Generally peaceful, although males will spar lightly. Shoaling fish, so keep at least five. Egg-layers. Eggs are deposited into the inhalant siphon of a mussel, often the Swan mussel Anodonta cygnea. Once hatched the fry are expelled from the mussel. Young Rosy Bitterling look plain and silvery, but the adults, especially the males, are gorgeously coloured. Other species occasionally available include the similar-looking **Taiwanese Bitterling** *Paracheilognathus himantegus*, and if bigger fish are your thing then the **Red China Rainbow** or **Giant Chinese Bitterling** *Acheilognathus macropterus* which can reach 27 cm (10.5 in). Bitterlings are difficult to breed because they need freshwater mussels to incubate their eggs, and these mussels are difficult to maintain in aquaria. Hence most Bitterling species are wild caught.

It is illegal to keep the **European Bitterling** *Rhodeus sericeus* in the UK.

Sharks

Shark is the common name given to a number of streamlined, high-dorsal-finned cyprinids. They are no relation to the marine sharks of 'Jaws' fame, being typically vegetarian, but some can be quite aggressive to similar-looking fish.

Red-tailed Black Shark
Epalzeorhynchus bicolor

Origin: Thailand
Length: 12 cm (4.7 in)
Lifespan: 8 years

Adult males are slimmer than females. An albino
variety is occasionally seen. Omnivores, but with heavy
leaning towards vegetarianism; will graze on algae,
but offer foods with increased greens included, such
as algae wafers. Tropical. Good water quality is a must,
otherwise the RTBS will appear grey with a pale tail.
These are not sociable fish and adults should be kept
singly in all but the largest aquarium. Keep only with
robust tank-mates such as cichlids, barbs and giant
danios. Egg-layer. Bred in their thousands on fish
farms in Thailand, the RTBS is IUCN listed as Extinct in
the Wild. The similar **Red-Finned** or **Rainbow Shark**
E. frenatus is slightly less aggressive and is
commonly available as a wild-type or
albino morph.

Flying Fox

Epalzeorhynchus kallopterus

Origin: Thailand, Malaysia and Indonesia
Length: 15 cm (6 in)
Lifespan: Over 10 years

Males are slimmer than females. Omnivores, but
with heavy leaning towards vegetarianism. They will
graze on algae, but offer foods with increased greens
included, such as algae wafers. Tropical. Good water
quality is a must. Adults are aggressive to each
other and sometimes to other, similar-looking fish.
Best kept individually except in very large aquaria.
Egg-layer. Rarely bred in aquaria. Often sold as
algae-eaters (they are actually not much better than
the preceding species, due to confusion with the
Siamese Algae Eater *Crossocheilus siamensis*. The
Siamese Algae Eater has a clear dorsal fin and a
single upper lip barbell, whereas the Flying Fox has
a striped dorsal and two barbels. The Siamese Algae
Eater grows to a similar size, is an excellent algae
consumer and can be kept in groups.

Silver Shark or Bala Shark

Balantiocheilos melanopterus

Origin: Borneo, Sumatra and possibly Malaysia
Length: 35 cm (14 in)
Lifespan: 8 to 19 years

Adult males slimmer than females. Omnivores,
but with heavy leaning towards vegetarianism; will
graze on algae, but offer foods with increased greens
included such as algae wafers. Tropical. Good water
quality essential. A sociable fish that should be kept in
small groups of five or more, which considering their
adult size will eventually demand a large aquarium
of at least 125 gallons. Peaceful towards other fish
too large to eat. Egg-layer; rarely bred by hobbyists.
Susceptible to white spot; good jumpers, so keep
aquarium covered. The Silver Shark is IUCN
listed as Endangered.

Loaches

Loaches are a group of bottom living cyprinids that are often thought of as janitors (alongside the many catfish species). However they all have specific needs.

Clown Loach
Chromobotia macracantha

Origin: Sumatra and Borneo
Length: 20 to 30 cm (8 to 12 in)
Lifespan: 15+ years

Adult females are larger and broader than males. Sexual maturity is at around 12 to 15 cm (4 to 6 in). Omnivores with a leaning towards carnivore; will eat usual foods. Will also eat snails, but should only be purchased for this task if you are prepared to meet its needs. Tropical. Good water quality is essential. Only introduce into established aquaria. Very sociable and lively. Best kept in groups of five or more; a large shoal would make a fascinating exhibit in a riverine setting.

Do not keep with fish which have long, flowing fins, such as male guppies. Egg layer. Attractive and boldly marked, these loaches do reach a significant size if cared for properly. They can make clicking noises when excited or agitated. There is a small spine situated just beneath the eye that can be erected if the loach feels threatened, such as when netted. Clown loaches and related species will often rest in the most bizarre of positions, something that can give concern when first observed. There are many related, similar-shaped loaches, all of which have similar requirements.

Oriental/Japanese Weather Loach or Dojo

Misgurnus augillicaudatus

Origin: Much of Asia including China, Korea, Laos and extending into Siberia

Length: 20 to 28 cm (8 to 11 in)

Lifespan: 10 years

Females are plumper; males have larger pectoral fins. Xanthic (golden) morph often available. Omnivores. Temperate. Needs good water quality. Very sociable with each other and no threat to other species, although it may hassle fancy varieties of goldfish. Egg layer. Does best in an aquarium with a sandy substrate where it can bury itself, leaving only its head showing. Said to be responsive to falling barometric pressure, becoming more active before rains – hence its common name. This can be an invasive species that has established itself in parts of southern Europe, the USA, Canada and Australia; legislation may cover the keeping of this fish in some of these countries. Weather loach can be quite susceptible to bacterial diseases.

Hillstream Loach, Butterfly Loach or Hong Kong Plec

Beaufortia kweichowensis

Origin: China
Length: 7.5 cm (2.9 in)
Lifespan: 6 years

Difficult to sex; adult females are broader with the snout forming a curve with the line of the pectoral fins. Males are slimmer, the snout is squarer and extends beyond the line of the pectoral fins. Herbivores with omnivorous tendencies; will eat usual foods and algae. In particular offer algae wafers or pellets. Temperate, but the related and similar-looking Gastromyzon sp from Borneo is tropical. Needs good water quality, highly-oxygenated. Peaceful with other fish, but can be territorial with each other. Egg-layer. Although often referred to as 'plecs', these fish are not related to the catfish of that name, but are in fact current-adapted loaches. Their body shape is extremely flattened, plus the fins fan out to form an enormous suction device to help these fish maintain position in the current. They are denizens of fast-flowing streams and do best in high-flow, rocky tanks that mimic their natural habitat. Aquaria with lower water turnover and reduced oxygenation are liable to significantly reduce their lifespan. Another attractive temperate Hill Stream Loach is the **Reticulated** or **Tiger Hillstream Loach** *Sewelia lineolata* from Vietnam.

Sucking Loach or Siamese Algae Eater
Gyrinocheilus aymonieri

Origin: Thailand and surrounding countries
Length: 28 cm (11 in)
Lifespan: 5 to 15 years

Adult males slimmer than females. Breeding males have tubercles on the snout. Xanthic (golden) morph and piebald individuals are seen. Herbivores with omnivorous tendencies; will eat usual foods and algae. In particular offer algae wafers or pellets. May attempt to feed on mucus direct from the fish, which can cause serious problems with larger, slow-moving fish such as angelfish or fancy goldfish. Tropical and temperate, Sucking Loaches are active over a wide range of temperatures, although tropical temperatures suit them best. Good water quality required. When small these loaches are cute and peaceful and will school together, but as they grow they become more aggressive and territorial both to each other and other fish.

Albino Sucking Loach

Image by © Ed Corp

Egg-layer. Sucking loach are readily available and are reasonably good at controlling nuisance algae, but if cared for correctly in time they become large and aggressive. In the right aquarium, around a 120 cm long, well-filtered tank with large and robust tank-mates, they can make suitable alternatives to sucking catfish, especially the colourful golden morph. The Sucking Loach is occasionally incorrectly sold as the Chinese Algae Eater.

Catfish

Catfish are a hugely popular, but often-misunderstood group of fish. Why misunderstood? Because some old books pitched them as janitors – fish whose main function was to clean up after the rest – that would snuffle out any uneaten bits of food, or clean algae off rocks, ornaments and the glass panes. They are so much more than this and represent a large and varied group of fish with extraordinary shapes, markings and behaviour. Buy a catfish because you want one, not because you want it to do something.

Corydoras Catfish

Corydoras Catfish are ideal community aquarium inhabitants. There is a wide variety of species available, and their care varies little between species. Commonly available species include:

Peppered Cory *Corydoras paleatus*
(normal, albino and long-finned).

Bronze Cory *Corydoras aeneus* (normal and albino).

Julii Cory *C. julii*

Bandit Cory *C. metae*

Panda Cory *C.panda*

Sterba's Cory *C. sterbai* (normal and albino).

Shwartz's Cory *C. shwartzi*

Spotted Cory *C. melanistius*

Dwarf Corydoras (average length 3 cm/1.2 in) includes the **Pygmy Cory** *C. pygmaeus* and **Dwarf Cory** *C. hastatus.*

Origin:	South America
Length:	7 to 8.5 cm (2.5 to 3.5 in)
Lifespan:	5 years+

Adult females are larger and plumper than adult males. Omnivores. Ensure food is the sinking type so these catfish get their fair share of, although they can make forays to the surface to eat floating flake.

Tropical, although the Peppered Corydoras is suitable for temperate aquaria. Good water quality a must. Keep on fine-grained gravel or river sand as coarse substrates can damage their delicate 'whiskers'. Very peaceful fish that are safe even with smaller species and young. Social fish, so best kept in groups of five or more. These are bottom living fish, but you will see them dart to the surface occasionally to take in a gulp of air. Egg-layers. Corydoras form a typical T-positioning while mating, following which the female presses the sticky eggs in small numbers on to firm surfaces. Corydoras are peaceful, but not defenceless. If attacked they lock their dorsal and pectoral fins out straight, which makes them literally difficult to swallow, and they may end up lodged in the mouth of large predators such as Oscars. The dwarf species are mid-water swimmers, unlike the other Corydoras.

Suckermouthed Catfish

Suckermouthed Catfish are members of the Loricaridae. They were originally utilised for their algae-eating appetites, but are now kept as much for their bizarre patterns and, on occasion, rarity appeal, as anything else. Surprisingly few are true herbivores – most are omnivores and some are carnivores/scavengers that will do little to reduce your algae.

Not all Suckermouthed Catfish have common names but most are given a number prefixed by the capital letter L until a valid name is decided upon.

The L stands for Loricarid. Some species have different colour or pattern morphs that may have different L-numbers, often because they were initially thought to represent distinct species. Hence the **Zebra Plec** *Hypancistrus zebra* is known as L046, but also L098 and L173.

Ancistrus or Bristlenose Catfish

Ancistrus cirrhosus

Origin: South America
Length: 12.5 cm (5 in)
Lifespan: 4 to 12 years

Mature males have multiple tentacle-like structures on head, plus spines (odontodes) on the cheeks and pectoral fins. Females may have some, but fewer than males. Normal, albino, calico and long-finned morphs. Herbivores with omnivorous tendencies; will eat usual foods and in particular, offer algae wafers or pellets. Will graze on algae. Small thin pieces of cucumber, suitably weighted, are also eaten. Tropical. Good water quality required. Generally an excellent tank-mate. Males may spar over territory, so make sure there are enough spawning caves available, and decorate the aquarium to obstruct lines of sight. Egg-layer. Cave spawner. Males tend the eggs and young. One of the best algal consumers, and does not grow too big.

Sailfin Plec, L083, L165
Pterygoplichthys gibbiceps

Origin: South America
Length: 45 cm (17.7 in)
Lifespan: 15 years

No obvious sex differences. Normal and albino available. Herbivore with omnivorous tendencies; will eat usual foods and algae. In particular, offer algae wafers or pellets. Large Sailfin Plecs need a lot of food and, unless specifically target fed, will become quite thin. Tropical. Good water quality essential, and good filtration required. Sailfin Plecs are relatively peaceful, but are well able to look after themselves. They can be territorial with other Sailfins. These catfish are excellent companions for large cichlids as they are heavily armoured, robust and aggressive enough to cope with the majority of cichlid attentions. Egg-layer. Males dig a tunnel into riverbanks in the wild and create a spawning chamber at the end. A stunning fish with its huge sail-like dorsal fin, but best left to those with super-sized aquaria. The same is also true of the related plecs such Hypostomus plecostomus which, although commonly available, will just grow too big if looked after correctly. This fish is also known as Glyptoperichthys gibbiceps.

Upside-Down Catfish

Synodontis nigriventris

Origin: Africa
Length: 10 cm (4 in)
Lifespan: 5 years

Adult males are slimmer and darker than mature females. Omnivores. Upside-Down catfish will feed from the surface...upside down! Tropical. Good water quality required. A peaceful fish that can be kept in groups. Egg-layer. Both parents tend the eggs and newly-hatched young. The colour shading on this fish is inverted to suit its unusual swimming position, with the underside darker than the back. Once free-swimming the young catfish assume a normal posture until around eight weeks of age, when they switch into upside-down mode. This unique catfish was known to the Egyptians.

Dwarf Suckermouth Catfish, Lda023

Otocinclus vittatus

Origin: South America
Length: 3.5 cm (1 4 in)
Lifespan: 5 years

No obvious sex differences. Herbivores with some omnivorous tendencies; will eat usual foods and algae. In particular offer algae wafers or pellets. Small thin pieces of cucumber, suitably weighted, are also eaten. Tropical. Good water quality essential. A peaceful catfish which shoals in the wild so always keep in a group of five or more. Egg-layer. No parental care. A diminutive catfish that is often quite fragile to begin with. Many specimens on sale appear in poor condition because their dietary needs are not catered for. The small size of this catfish makes it ideal for nano-aquaria or heavily planted tanks, where it can feed on algae-coated plants leaves but causes little damage.

Glass Catfish
Kryptopterus minor

Origin: South-east Asia
Length: 8 cm (3.2 in)
Lifespan: 8 years

No obvious sex differences. Carnivores. May need to offer small live foods initially. Tropical. Very sensitive to poor water quality. Appreciates reasonable water flow to mimic its riverine natural habitat. It is a very peaceful and delicate fish and is at risk of being bullied by more assertive fish, such as cichlids and barbs. Keep in a small school of at least six. Singles and pairs will often waste away without company. Prefers an aquarium with some floating plants to enhance its feelings of security. Egg-layer. A transparent fish is a novelty and the muscles of this fish are aligned to cause minimal light absorption or refraction, so that light can pass through unhindered. The skeleton is still visible, as are the eyes and the body cavity that houses the internal organs.

Clown Pleco
L104, L162 Lda022
Panaque maccus

Origin: South America
Length: 10 cm (4 in)
Lifespan: 10 to12 years

Breeding males develop small spines (odontodes) on the cheeks. Herbivores with omnivorous tendencies; will eat usual foods and algae. In particular, offer algae wafers or pellets. Small thin pieces of cucumber, suitably weighted, are also eaten. Has an absolute need for bogwood or similar to chew on, as do other Panaque species. Tropical. Good water quality essential. Peaceful. Can be kept in small groups. Egg-layer; cave spawner. Clown Plecs are a small, attractively striped catfish that can be kept in small groups. Not too good at algae-eating duties however, so choose it for its own sake.

Image by
© Gary McKinney

Characins

Characins are a large group of shoaling fish with strongholds in South America and Africa. The most popular groups are the **Tetras** that contain some of the most attractive and sought-after fish in the hobby. Fortunately their care differs little between species and, with a few exceptions, they can be discussed together.

Small tetras

Many species of tetras are regularly available, and some favourites are given here. Probably the most popular species are those with highly reflective stripes that extend all or part way along the body of the fish.

- **Neon Tetra** *Paracheirodon innesi* (including Diamond and semi-albino Gold forms)

- **Cardinal Tetra** *Paracheirodon axelrodi*

- **Green Neon Tetra** *Paracheirodon simulans*

- **Glowlight Tetra** *Hemigrammus erythrozonus* (including albino form)

- **Black Neon Tetra** *Hyphessobrycon herbertaxelrodi*

- **Emperor Tetra** *Nematobrycon palmeri*

Other small but colourful tetras are:

- **Black Phantom Tetras** *Hyphessobrycon megalopterus*

- **Red Phantom Tetras** *Hyphessobrycon sweglesi*

- **Lemon Tetras** *Hyphessobrycon pulchripinnis*

- **Flame Tetras** *Hyphessobrycon flammeus*

- **Penguins** *Thayeria boehlkei*

- **Columbian Tetra** *Hyphessobrycon columbianus*

- **Red-Eyed Tetra** *Moenkhausia sanctaefilomenae*

- **Bloodfin** *Aphyocharax anisitsi*

- **Rummy-Nosed Tetra** *Hemigrammus rhodostomus* and similar species.

Serpae Tetras
Hyphessobrycon eques

Origin: South America
Length: Up to 3 cm (1.2 in)
Lifespan: 5 to 10 years

Mature males are generally slimmer, while females have a more rounded body shape. Microcarnivores that will take usual foods. Tropical (but see later). Good water quality essential. With very few exceptions all of these fish are compatible both with members of their own species and others. For best visual impact keep a large shoal of a single species rather than a mixed group.

Do not keep with fish large enough to eat them! Egg-layer; egg scatterer. These fish are one of the mainstays of tropical fishkeeping. Most are captive-bred in huge numbers in Asia, but some, such as the Cardinal Tetra, are still routinely wild caught.

Regularly available. These are gorgeous fish that have a rust to red body colour with black markings, but they have a major drawback in being serious fin-nippers. As a result they are best kept either in a species aquarium or with fast, robust and short-finned fish.

Large tetras

There are some large tetras and related characins regularly available.

- **Buenos Aires Tetra** *Hyphessobrycon anisitsi* (normal and albino)

- **Black Widow Tetra** or **Black Skirt Tetra** *Gymnocorymbus ternetzi* (many varieties including long-finned)

- **Congo Tetra** *Phenacogrammus interruptus* (including albino)

- **Silver Dollars** *Metynnis hypsauchen and M. argentus* can be included in this list because, although not tetras, these characins need similar, albeit scaled up, care.

Origin: Congo Tetra (Africa); Silver Dollar, Black Widow and Buenos Aires Tetra (South America)

Length: Tetras up to 8 cm (3.2 in); Silver Dollars 15 cm (6 in)

Lifespan: 5 to 10 years

Male Congo Tetras have longer fins with extensions; in Silver Dollars, the anal fin is more elongated and colourful in males. Omnivores. Silver Dollars and Buenos Aires Tetras are highly herbivorous and will decimate soft-leaved plants in a planted tank.

Tropical (but see later). Good water quality required. These characins are large, but social and best kept in shoals.

In large aquaria they make excellent dither fish for larger tank-mates such as cichlids. Buenos Aires Tetras can be fin-nippers so best kept with short-finned, active fish. Egg-layer; egg-scatterer. The large size of these fish and their social nature mean that a large aquarium with good filtration is a necessity.

Some of the tetras listed above are found as far south as the Tropic of Capricorn and beyond, which makes them suitable candidates for temperate aquaria. These tetras are Bloodfins, Flame Tetras, Black Widows and Buenos Aires Tetras.

Blind Cavefish
Astyanax mexicanus

Origin: Mexico
Length: 9 cm (3.6 in)
Lifespan: 5 years +

Adult males are slimmer with a more obvious curved edge to the anal fin. Cave morph and normal (sighted). Omnivore. Tropical. Good water quality essential. Relatively peaceful, although they can be fin nippers so avoid keeping with slow or long-finned fish. These tetras do not school and their swimming pattern

Image by
© Ron DeCloux

can seem quite frenetic. Species aquaria mimicking caverns using rockwork, black gravel and spotlighting can be extremely effective. Egg-scatterer. The Blind Cave Tetra is a cave-adapted morph of the **Mexican Tetra**. In evolutionary terms it has adapted to its dark natural habitat by losing its eyes (although they are present at hatching) and compensating by enhancing its other senses, such as the lateral line. This helps the fish to navigate obstacles by sensing pressure differences in the surrounding water.

Marbled Hatchetfish
Carnegiella strigata

Origin:	South America
Length:	4 cm (1.6 in)
Lifespan:	5 years

Females deeper bodied than males, especially when breeding. Microcarnivores, but can also be fed small live foods such as Drosophila fruit flies. Tropical. Good water quality essential. Peaceful. Spends most of its time at the surface. Keep in covered aquaria as it may jump and 'fly' if startled - for example by the sudden switching on of lights in a darkened room. Egg-scatterer. This is a genuine flying fish. The wing-like pectoral fins have enlarged muscles attached to them, which beat these fins like wings, giving some element of powered flight.

This beating can produce a buzzing sound as the fish flies through the air. This is an escape tactic designed to confuse aquatic predators – the fish will literally disappear from a predator's sight, leaving no clue as to which direction it went!

Red-Bellied Piranha
Pygocentrus nattereri

Origin: South America
Length: 30 cm (12 in)
Lifespan: 10 years

No obvious sex differences. 'Super reds' occasionally available. Related Pygocentrus species (P. caribe and P. piraya) occasionally offered for sale. Omnivores with carnivorous tendencies; can be trained to take pelleted and frozen foods (fish, prawns, squid etc). There is no requirement to feed live fish. Tropical. Good water quality essential. Either keep one, or keep five or more. Piranhas are a naturally shoaling species, but each individual likes its space, and aggression is regularly seen in groups. In the confines of all but the largest aquaria this aggression can have serious consequences – piranha can quickly do a lot of damage to each other and fish with bite-wounds and missing eyes are common.

In larger schools this aggression is dispersed; in pairs or trios the usual outcome is just one dominant individual. Breeding males are especially aggressive. Other tank-mates, with the occasional exception of either large Plecostomus catfish or small tetras such as Neon Tetras, will be eaten. Egg-layer. Males will excavate a basic nest and guard the eggs and fry until they are free-swimming.

Piranhas have a fearsome reputation but in captivity are often nervous and flighty. The Red-bellied piranha is often confused with the **Red-Breasted Pacu** Piaractus brachypomus. This piranha mimic (possibly so it can associate with piranha unmolested) grows huge (60 cm/24 in or more) but unlike its piranha cousins, is vegetarian. The Red-bellied Piranha is potentially quite an invasive species. It is illegal to keep piranha in any of the southern USA states, whilst in others it may be only legal to keep them with a permit, so it is best to check the local laws. It is illegal to keep piranha in Australia, although some states may allow this under permit. Again contact the local authorities.

Cichlids

Cichlids are a diverse and successful group of fish with particular strongholds in Africa, Central and South America. These fish are popular for their bright colours and complex behaviour patterns. Care for their young is typical. This can vary between species from mouth-brooding of eggs and young (either by the male or female), maternal care of the young or biparental by the mother and father. This care can be aggressive; pairs with young may try to exclude all other fish from their breeding territory, often causing havoc in a previously peaceful aquarium.

Angelfish
Pterophyllum scalare

Origin: South America

Length: 15 cm (6 in) but up to 20 cm (8 in) tall

Lifespan: 10 years

Males are more aggressive. When spawning the genital tube is thin and pointed in males, thicker and rounder in females. Colour varieties include zebra, black, gold, marble, koi and albino. Physical morphs would include veiltails and pearlscales. Carnivores. Tropical. Otherwise good water quality. A good community fish with similar sized, quiet fish. Schooling fish except when breeding. Large angelfish may eat small fish such as Neon Tetras. Egg-layer; bi-parental family. Angelfish are the archetypal tropical fish. Elegant and beautiful it is easy to forget that these are carnivores and can be relatively aggressive. Unlike many cichlids these are compatible with planted aquaria.

Discus
Symphysodon hybrids

Origin: South America
Length: 14- 22.5 cm. (4- 9 in)
Lifespan: 10 to 18 years

Adult males have slightly longer fins and may have a slight doming of the head (nuchal hump). When spawning the genital tube is thin and pointed in males, thicker and rounder in females. There are three species of discus – Symphysodon discus, S. aequifasciatus and S. haraldi. Most of the commercially available discus varieties are hybrids of two or more of these. Discus have become a true hobby fish with a vast number of colours available. Examples include Turquoise, Snakeskin, Pigeonblood, Red, White and Albino. There are some high-bodied breeds too. Carnivore. High tropical temperatures of 26-31°C (79 to 88F). Soft water of low pH (6.0-7.0) preferred. Water quality must be good. A highly sociable and mild-mannered fish when not breeding. Can be kept with a variety of fish that are able to tolerate the high temperatures needed by Discus. Often combined to good effect with Cardinal and Rummynose Tetras. Egg-layer; bi-parental spawner. Both sexes produce nutritious skin mucus on which the young discus are initially fed.

Stunning colours and fascinating breeding behaviour mean that discus are always popular, but they are not for beginners. Wild-caught discus are especially sensitive and disease-prone and should be left to experienced hobbyists. However if you provide the high temperatures and good water quality needed the commercial strains are surprisingly hardy and tolerant. Stunning planted species aquaria can be created.

Ram or Butterfly Dwarf Cichlid

Mikrogeophagus ramirezi

Origin: South America
Length: 5 cm (2 in)
Lifespan: 4 years

Adult males generally have a larger body, longer fins and brighter colours. Golden and Electric Blue colour varieties. Physical morphs include long-finned and balloon-body. Omnivores. Tropical. Good water quality essential. Rams are compatible with small community fish such as tetras. Egg-layer. Bi-parental family. Rams are a beautiful cichlid but be warned – they are often not very hardy. Similar fish offered for sale include the Bolivian Ram M. altispinosa and the unrelated African Butterfly Cichlid Anomalochromis thomasi. The care for all three is identical.

The Krib or Kribensis

Pelvicachromis pulcher

Origin: Africa
Length: Males 10 cm (4 in) Females 7.5 cm (3 in)
Lifespan: 5 years

Males are larger and longer than females with more pointed fins. Females have a more rounded appearance and the abdomen turns purple when ready to breed. Albino available. Several other Pelvicachromis species are occasionally available. Omnivores. Tropical. Good water quality essential. Pairs will aggressively defend their young, but if the aquarium is large enough then this causes few problems. Egg-layer that spawns in caves. Bi-parental family. Sex ratio is affected by pH – lower pH will give more females, higher pH more males, so aim for 6.5- 7.0. Kribs are excellent beginner cichlids as they are moderate sized, colourful and breed easily and dependably.

Parrot Cichlid
Cichlasoma hybrid

Origin: Man-made. Possibly originating from a cross between two Central American cichlids – the **Midas Cichlid** *Amphiiophus citrinellus* and the **Quetzel Cichlid** *Vieja synspilus*; others suggest the second parent was the **Severum** *Heros efasciatus*

Length: 25 cm (10 in)

Lifespan: 10 years

Adult males may be slimmer. When spawning the genital tube is thin and pointed in males, thicker and rounder in females. The Parrot Cichlid is usually available as either an orange or yellow colour. Some naturally patterned varieties, for example Kirin or Bonsai Flowerhorns, are sometimes seen. Occasionally dyed or even tattooed individuals are found, but such modified fish are unethical, represent a welfare problem and are possibly illegally offered for sale in the UK under the Animal Welfare Act 2006. Omnivores. Tropical. Good water quality essential. Compatible with robust medium to large sized fish. These fish still have the aggressive tendencies of their parental species, but the poorly formed shape of the mouth means that their ability to damage is reduced. Egg-layer; biparental family, but males are often infertile.

Will cross with other Central American cichlids. These fish are hugely controversial, not only because of their origins, but because of the mutations that are fixed and reproduced (deformed mouth and shortened body) and the further physical modifications such as artificial colour-dyeing that sometimes are inflicted on these fish. Other hybrid cichlids, also controversial, are the Flowerhorns (or Hua Luo Han). Flowerhorns are big, aggressive cichlids that require an aquarium to themselves. Note that there is a true Parrot Cichlid Hoplarchus psittacus that is native to South America but is rarely seen in the hobby.

Oscar
Astronotus ocellatus

Origin:　South America
Length:　Typically 30 cm (12 in) but
　　　　　　potentially larger
Lifespan:　10 to 18 years

Generally impossible to distinguish between the sexes, but when spawning the genital tube is thin and pointed in males, thicker and rounder in females. Tiger, albino and red colour morphs plus veiltail. Omnivores.Tropical. Needs good water quality and such a large fish can put a strain on the filtration system. May also attack and break heaters, so either situate these outside the aquarium or protect them with commercial heater guards. When not breeding, fine with fish too large to swallow (and they have big mouths). Best kept singly or as a compatible pair. Egg-layer. Bi-parental family. If you want a large, responsive pet fish then this is the one for you. Commonly considered to be one of the most intelligent fish kept in aquaria, they will rapidly learn who their owner is and beg for food. Avoid impulse buying of the cute babies as they will rapidly decimate your community aquarium; only buy if you can give them a large tank, a big filter and a commitment for a decade or more. If you do, you will be rewarded...big time!

Convict Cichlid
Amatitlania nigrofasciata

Origin: Central America
Length: Adult males 15 cm (6 in)
Lifespan: 10 to 18 yrs

Adult males are larger, have longer fins and a slight nuchal hump. Females are much smaller and have orangey-bronze coloured scales on the belly. Leucistic (white) and calico. Blue convicts are probable hybrids with Honduran Red Points. Omnivores. Tropical. Prefer harder water but will adapt to most waters. Good water quality essential. Keep only with large and very robust fish. Convict cichlids are aggressive, especially when they have young, and they breed very easily. Keep either in a species aquarium or with larger cichlids, giving the Convicts multiple rocky caves to hide and breed in. Egg-layers; Bi-parental family. Cave spawners. Convict Cichlids may be small for Central American cichlids, but they are uncompromisingly aggressive. It is easy to be negative about Convicts but in truth they are attractive and have fascinating behaviour patterns. They breed easily so are readily available. The closely related **Honduran Red Point** *A. siquia* has similar body stripes but overlain on a blue body, with reddish fins. They are considered to be less aggressive than Convicts.

Rift Lake Cichlids are a fascinating group of African cichlids found in the Rift Lakes, namely Lakes Malawi, Tanganyika and Victoria. These lakes are in fact inland seas of freshwater that harbour huge and complex species flocks. The waters here are very hard (200 to 220 mg/l $CaCO_3$ Hardness) and of high ph – typically around pH 8.0 or higher for Tanganyika. Many of these cichlids, especially Malawis, are highly coloured but they are also very aggressive. Aggression is best managed by heavy stocking levels that prevent the easy establishment of territory, plus multiple rocky hiding places that mimic their natural habitat.

Be wary about buying fish from tanks labelled 'Mixed Malawi Cichlids' or similar – you should know what species you are buying, and the females of many species look similar. Hybridisation can occur quite easily within some species groups.

Electric Yellow Labidochromis

Labidochromis caeruleus

Origin: Lake Malawi, Africa
Length: 7.5 cm (3 in)
Lifespan: 10 years

Adult males are slightly larger and develop black/ blue in the anal and pectoral fins. There are several naturally occurring colour morphs. Yellow (or Lion's Cove), white and white with blue fins. Omnivore; will eat usual foods, with emphasis on spirulina and algae wafers. Tropical. Rift Lake values (see above). Good water quality essential. A peaceful fish in an otherwise aggressive group. Best kept with other moderately peaceful Malawi cichlids in a dedicated aquarium. Maternal mouthbrooder. The Yellow Labidochromis is relatively peaceful, with the bright yellow colouration of the Lion's Cove morph, making it very popular. Best kept as a trio or five with only one male, unless the aquarium is very large. Keep the different colour morphs, and related Labidochromis species, separate as they will readily hybridise.

Auratus or Golden Mbuna
Melanochromis auratus

Origin: Lake Malawi, Africa
Length: 9 cm (3.5 in)
Lifespan: 5 to 9 years

Adult females are a golden colour with two dark
horizontal stripes; adult males are almost the
negative of this, being largely black with one lighter
horizontal stripe. Omnivores; will eat usual foods,
with emphasis on spirulina and algae wafers.
Tropical. Rift Lake values (see above). Good water
quality essential. A very aggressive fish, best kept
in a specific Malawi aquarium with other Malawi
cichlids. Maternal mouthbrooder. Keep as a group
(one male, two or more females), but the aquarium
must be large as females are not tolerant of each
other. Provide plenty of rocky caves and obstacles to
break up the lines of sight in the aquarium.

Red Zebra
Pseudotropheus estherae

Origin: Lake Malawi, Africa
Length: 11.5 cm (4 in)
Lifespan: 10 years

In some populations the males are blue while the females are bright orange. Where the sexes are the same colour, adult males are larger than females and have more 'egg-spots' on the anal fin. There are several geographic colour varieties; the blue male/orange female type is usually available, but orange or orange blotch (OB) males are seen, as are yellow or OB females. Omnivores; will eat usual foods, with emphasis on spirulina and algae wafers. Tropical. Rift Lake values (see above). Otherwise good water quality. Moderately aggressive. Best kept in a dedicated Malawi aquarium. Maternal mouthbrooder; cave spawner. The eye-catching colours of this fish have made it popular, but it is not suitable for a normal community aquarium. Do not keep with closely related 'Zebras', including Metriaclima and Maylandia species.

Brichardi or Fairy Cichlid
Neolamprologus brichardi

Origin: Lake Tanganyika, Africa
Length: 10 cm (4 in)
Lifespan: 10 years

Adult males are slightly larger with longer fin extensions. Albinos available. Omnivores. Tropical. Rift Lake values (see above). Good water quality essential. Relatively peaceful, but parents can be aggressive when defending young. Best kept in groups. Egg-layer; Biparental family. Cave spawner. The young from previous spawnings will stay with the parents and help to co-operatively defend their parents' territory, along with the latest brood. Although not brightly coloured, this cichlid has a certain elegance with its muted colours and lyre-shaped tail. Family comes first with this fish and in the wild huge shoals of related individuals will defend their territory.

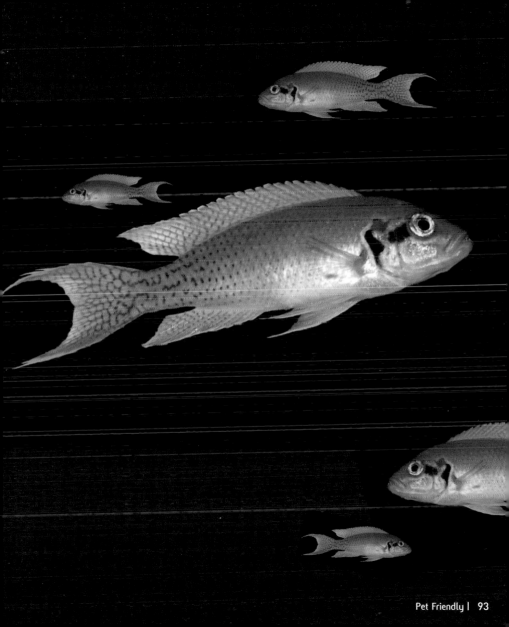

Anabantids

The **Anabantids** are a group of African and Asian fish that contains some of the most popular aquarium species. Most of those commonly kept have evolved in shallow, warm and sluggish water conditions. Adaptations to these environments typically include an ability to breathe atmospheric air and the building by the male of a raft-like bubblenest, where the eggs are placed and tended in the relatively high oxygen environment at the surface.

Three Spot Gourami
Trichogaster trichopterus

Origin:	South-east Asia
Length:	15 cm (6 in)
Lifespan:	4 years

Adult males are slimmer and have a larger, more pointed dorsal fin. Blue, golden, platinum and lavender morphs as well as the original wild brown. The Cosby morph is light blue with large, dark blue-to-black patches overlying. Omnivores. Tropical. Good water quality essential. Peaceful when young, but some individuals can be aggressive as adults. Keep with similar-sized fish. Bubblenest builder. A very hardy fish available in some stunning colour morphs. Outside of Malawi cichlids it is difficult to find other such blue fish.

Pearl Gourami
Trichogaster leeri

Origin: South-east Asia
Length: 12 cm (4.8 in)
Lifespan: 5 years+

Mature males have larger fins, with the dorsal fin being especially elongated. The breast is suffused with an orangey-red colour. Omnivores. Tropical. Good water quality essential. Relatively peaceful for a large gourami – do not keep with aggressive or fin-nipping tank-mates. Keep only one male unless the aquarium is large. Bubblenest builder. This is a beautiful and graceful fish. The net-like markings and the draping fins of the male give a lace-like appearance.

In breeding males this effect is enhanced by the suffused pinkish-orange of the chest to produce a truly stunning fish.

Dwarf Gourami
Colisa lalia

Origin: India
Length: 7.5 cm (3 in)
Lifespan: 4 years

Males generally very colourful, while females are drabber. Red, blue, metallic (neon) varieties. Omnivores. Tropical. Good water quality essential. A good community fish and small enough to keep several males in a moderate sized aquarium. Shoaling fish when not breeding, generally well behaved with other fish species. Bubblenest builder. Males of all varieties are gorgeous, but buy these fish with caution. Modern strains appear to be very prone to disease, especially fish tuberculosis and iridovirus. Other similar gouramies are the **Honey Gourami** *C. chuna* and the **Red Robin Gourami**, which actually appears to be a hybrid between the Honey Gourami and the **Thick-Lipped Gourami** *C. labiosa*.

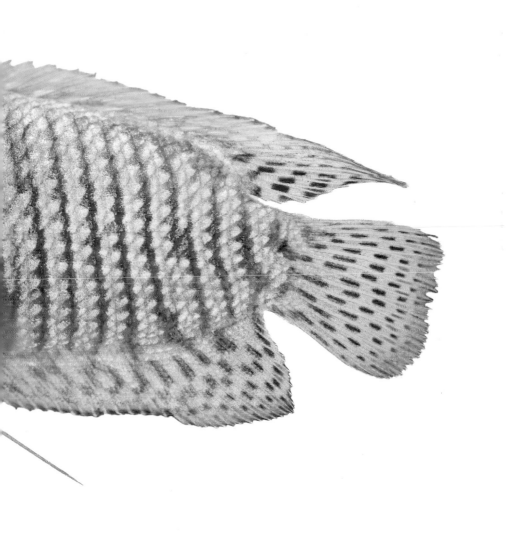

Siamese Fighting Fish
Betta splendens

Origin: South-east Asia
Length: 6 to 7 cm (2.5 to 3 in)
Lifespan: 2 years

Males have longer fins; the veiltail variety is 'industry standard' where the males have extensively developed finnage. Mature females are more rounded with a white ovipositor visible at the vent. There is an infinite variety of colour morphs including blue, green, red, butterfly, tricolour and Cambodian (cream with red fins). Physical morphs are largely limited to the finnage and include veiltail, halfmoon, crowntail and rosetail. Hybridisation with the closely related Betta mahachai has produce the highly reflectile, armour-like scales seen on 'dragon' fighters. Carnivores, but will eat the usual foods. Tropical, towards the high end of range (25-30°C). Good water quality essential. Two adult males will spar intensely, which in a small space can lead to the death of one. The aquarium strains were originally developed from fighting lines and have increased aggressive tendencies, exacerbated by the solitary way the males are traditionally reared.

Males may also attack closely-related species including smaller gouramies, and long-finned fish such as male guppies. The long-finned varieties prove easy targets for fin nippers such as barbs. Females can be kept together in groups and with other typical community species. Their small size and stunning colours make them ideal for nano-aquaria.

Bubble nest builder. Originally domesticated for fighting (gambling) purposes, Siamese Fighting Fish are now a hobby fish with an enormous following. Fighters are as often sinned against as sinners themselves. Males are reared individually in small containers and the long-finned varieties in particular can find life in a normal community aquarium difficult. Siamese Fighting Fish can be kept in small aquaria, but room temperature is often too low for these fish in temperate climates, so accessory heating is a must.

Paradise Fish
Macropodus opercularis

Origin: Southern China and Eastern Asia
Length: 10 cm (4 in)
Lifespan: 8 years

Adult males have greatly elongated fins. Females are less brightly coloured and often plumper. Red, blue and albino varieties available. Omnivores. Tropical and temperate. Good water quality essential. Males will spar aggressively, and may hassle gentler fish such as goldfish. Otherwise fine with similar sized, robust fish such as Rosy Barbs and American Flagfish. A male/female pair will do well in a medium-sized species aquarium. Happiest at room temperature. Bubble nest builder. Paradise Fish get an unjustifiable bad press. Happy at room temperature, these are the ideal fish for a small bedroom aquarium. Adult males have beautiful flowing fins with red and blue alternating body stripes. They quickly learn to recognise their owner and can be readily taught to jump for their favourite food of bloodworm.

After goldfish, these were the first true 'tropical'
fish and are thought to be fish referred to by
Samuel Pepys in 1665 as 'fishes kept in a glass of
water, that will live so forever, and finely marked
they are, being foreign'. Keep a paradise fish
and you keep a piece of aquarium history.
Only adult males, of length greater than 6
cm, are permitted for sale in Australia.

Livebearers

Livebearers are an extremely popular group of fish, both because of their bright colours and the fact that they give birth to fully-formed and easily rearable young. Many species of fish give birth to live young, including the Great White Shark! The commonest ones encountered by fishkeepers are the Poecilids such as guppies, mollies and swordtails, and the Goodeids.

Guppy

Poecilia reticulata

Origin: Central America, northern South America and the Caribbean. Introduced elsewhere for mosquito control

Length: Males around 3 cm (1.2 in) females up to 5 cm (2 in)

Lifespan: Potentially three to five years, but many modern varieties seldom survive longer than 18 months

Mature males are more colourful and the anal fin is modified into a pointed gonopodium. Adult females are usually quite dull coloured and rounded. There are literally hundreds of domestic varieties of guppies, including pedigree lines of show guppies. Hypomelanistic (blonde) individuals are also available. Omnivore. Tropical. Good water quality essential. Social fish, best kept in groups. Males constantly court females so it is better to keep more females than males to reduce harassment. Veiltail males may be targeted by barbs and male bettas. Females will produce broods of 20 to 30 babies every four to six weeks, although large females can produce well over 100 at a time.

The wild guppy is a small, fairly drab fish, but selective breeding has produced guppies of increased size, gorgeous colouring and a variety of tail shapes. In some lines even the females sport tail colours. Originally quite hardy, modern guppy varieties are less robust and more disease prone. They will do best in a species aquarium, or with a few mild-mannered companions, but with the colours available – what a display that could be! The closely related **Endler's Livebearer** Poecilia wingei is smaller and will hybridise with the Guppy.

Mollies
Poecilia hybrids

Origin: Depending upon species of origin, from coastal southern USA, Atlantic coasts of Central America and northern South America

Length: From 6 cm (2.4 in) in short-finned sphenops-like males to 18 cm (7 in) for female sailfin-types

Lifespan: Up to 4 years

Mature males are slimmer and the anal fin is modified into a pointed gonopodium. Adult females are usually larger and more rounded. There are many colour varieties ranging from jet black to bright orange. Physical morphs include lyretails and sail-fins, plus short-bodied types (balloon mollies). Omnivores. They will graze on algae and should be offered foods designed for herbivorous fish. Tropical, preferably towards the higher end of the range (25 to 28°C). Appreciate hard water and often do better in slightly brackish (low levels of salt) water. Good water quality essential. Social, although males may display aggressively to one another. A species aquarium that provides them with high temperatures, water hardness and salt levels would be ideal. Some 40 to 80 young born every five to seven weeks. Most commercially available mollies are hybrids of several different species including the Liberty molly (P. sphenops), the Giant Sailfin molly (P. velifera) and the Sailfin molly (P. latipinna). Of these only the Giant Sailfin is ever seen with any regularity in aquarium stores. Mollies are pickier about their water quality than many fish. Lower temperatures, soft water and lack of salt can make them susceptible to disease. Avoid buying those fish that display shimmying (exaggerated swimming-on-the-spot movements, often with clamped fins) as these are ill.

Swordtails
Xiphophorus helleri

Origin: Central America

Length: Males up to 10 cm (4 in) excluding sword and females up to 12 cm (4.7 in)

Lifespan: 3 to 5 years

Mature males are slimmer and the anal fin is modified into a pointed gonopodium. Adult females are usually larger and more rounded. Although sexually mature males do develop a 'sword' (formed from the extended lower rays of the caudal fin) this is not always well developed. Some males are late developers and will appear female for quite some time. Some elderly females may develop this secondary male characteristic due to hormonal changes. There are many colour varieties including albino, plus some physical morphs such as hi-fin (enlarged dorsal fin), Simpson (elongated finnage) and double sword. Omnivores. Tropical. Prefer harder water, but otherwise good water quality. A medium-sized good, robust community fish. Males can be aggressive to each other so only keep one in smaller aquaria. Large females can produce 100 or more young every 4 to 6 weeks.

Although only males carry a sword, in many varieties
this is much shorter than the wild-type form,
probably because there has been much interbreeding
with the Platy (X. maculatus) and the Variatus platy
(X. variatus).

Platy & Variatus Platy
Xiphophorus maculatus & X. variatus

Origin: Central America

Length: Variatus males up to 5.5 cm (2.2 in) and females larger at 7 cm (2.8 in). X maculatus is generally smaller than X. variatus

Lifespan: 3 to 5 years

Mature males are slimmer and the anal fin is modified into a pointed gonopodium. Adult females are usually larger and more rounded. There are a huge number of colour varieties of both species and their hybrids, plus crosses with Swordtails. Physical morphs include hi-fins (enlarged dorsal fins) and small swords on the tail-fin. Omnivores; will graze on algae. Tropical. Variatus platies can be kept in temperate aquaria too. Prefer hard water. Good water quality essential. Social fish best kept in mixed sex groups. Broods of 40 to 50 or more are produced every 4 to 6 weeks. Platies can be good, all round community fish. There is a deep red version of the Platy known as 'coral red' which is stunning, especially when kept as a group. The natural form of the Variatus Platy is particularly attractive too.

Butterfly Goodeid

Ameca splendens

Origin: Mexico

Length: Females up to 12 cm (4.7 in), males smaller

Lifespan: 5 years

Males have a notched anal fin. Omnivore. Will graze algae. Tropical. Good water quality essential. Compatibility: Can be aggressive and a fin nipper. Groups will form hierarchies, with the dominant male showing the brightest colours. Best kept either as a species aquarium or with larger, robust fish such as barbs. 6 to 40 young are born at intervals of eight weeks or more. The Butterfly Goodeid is IUCN listed as Extinct in the Wild. They are reasonably available in the hobby and, by keeping them, you are doing your bit for their conservation.

Image by
© Ron DeCloux

Miscellaneous

Black Knife Fish
Apteronotus albifrons

Origin: Amazonia
Length: Potentially up to 50 cm (20 in)
Lifespan: 8 to 10 years

No obvious sex differences. Carnivores. Will take live
and frozen foods, but may be weaned on to dried foods
given time. Tropical. Good water quality essential. Can be
aggressive with others of its own species, therefore keep
either singly or in a group in a large (200 cm) aquarium.
Timid, but large specimens may eat smaller fish. Egg-layer;
farmed commercially. This is a large fish, so when buying
one plan accordingly. Black Knife Fish generate a
weak electrical field around themselves, which
they use to navigate by and identify
individuals.

Image by
© Shadowshador

Dwarf Pufferfish

Carinotetraodon travancoricus

Origin: India
Length: 2.5 cm (1 in)
Lifespan: 2 to 5 years

Adult males often have a dark mid-line streak running along their underside, plus lines that resemble wrinkles behind the eyes. Carnivores that prefer live or frozen foods such as bloodworm, daphnia and brine shrimp. Tropical. Unlike many other pufferfish offered for sale, such as the Figure-Eight Puffer Tetraodon biocellatus, these are completely freshwater and therefore do not require any salt. Good water quality essential. Dwarf puffers can be aggressive fin nippers, so avoid keeping with long-finned fish or slow swimmers. They will do best in a mixed sex group in a well-planted species aquarium. Egg layer. Dwarf puffers are cuteness personified with huge characters. Suitable for nano-aquaria.

Senegal or Cuvier's Birchir
Polypterus senegalis

Origin: Africa
Length: 50 cm (20 in)
Lifespan: 10 to 30 years

Males have a thicker anal fin. Albino morph also available. Carnivores that will eat any fish they can fit in their mouths. Nocturnal hunters, so do not be fooled by day-time nonchalance. Tropical. Good water quality essential. Good community fish with larger, robust fish that cannot be eaten. Egg-layers. The polypterids are an ancient lineage of fish dating back to the time of the dinosaurs. Sometimes they appear to walk along the substrate using their pectoral fins as 'legs'. Birchirs are also able to breathe air gulped in at the surface.

Golden Wonder Panchax
Aplochcilus lineatus

Origin: Sri Lanka and southern India
Length: 10 cm (4 in)
Lifespan: 3 years

Adult males are larger and more brightly coloured than females. The Golden Wonder Panchax is a selectively-bred morph of the Striped Panchax. Omnivores. Tropical. Good water quality essential. A peaceful surface dweller if kept with fish too large to eat, it is a carnivore that will feed on smaller fish. Can be aggressive to each other but in medium to large aquaria can be kept in groups. Egg-scatterer. Excellent jumper so aquarium must be covered.

American Flagfish

Jordanella floridae

Origin: Southern USA coast from Florida to Yucatan Peninsula

Length: 6 cm (2.25 in)

Lifespan: 3+ years (longer at lower temperatures)

Adult males are larger and have green spangling on red base colour. The smaller females have an obvious dark patch on the dorsal fin. Omnivores. An avid algal grazer. Tropical and temperate. Good water quality essential. Can be kept in groups in larger aquaria, but males can be aggressive, especially when spawning. Flagfish can be occasional fin-nippers, so avoid keeping with long-finned fish. Egg layer. Can alternate between egg-scattering and paternal egg care. A great fish for an unheated aquarium that is both colourful and useful for algae control. Do not keep with fancy goldfish.

Invertebrates

Freshwater shrimps

Unlike in the marine fishkeeping hobby, the keeping of freshwater invertebrates for their beauty rather than as utilitarian creatures, is a relatively new thing.

Ornamental **Shrimps** have a significant following today. A combination of selective breeding for colour, increased availability of species, the rise in popularity of nano-aquaria and, in the case of Amano shrimps, their use in algae control, has lead to a rapid increase in popularity.

- **Crystal Shrimp** *Caridina cf. cantonensis sp.* "Crystal Red".

- **Algae-Eating** or **Amano Shrimp** *Caridina multidentata (sometimes C. japonica).*

- **Cherry Shrimp** *Neocaridina denticulata sinensis.*

- **Bamboo Shrimp** *Atyopsis moluccensis.*

- **African Filter** or **Vampire Shrimp** *Atya gabonensis.*

Origin: Japan, Taiwan and China. The African Filter Shrimp, not surprisingly, comes from Africa.

Length: Up to 5 cm (2 in) for Amano shrimp while the Bamboo and African Filter Shrimps can reach 12 cm (4.7 in).

Lifespan: 3 to 5 years

Adult males smaller than females. 'Berried' females are those that are carrying bunches of eggs under the abdomen. The Crystal Red Shrimp is a variety of the Bee Shrimp (C. cantonensis).

Other Caridina and Neocaridina species are becoming available. Omnivores. Many will feed on any organic material in the aquarium, including algae. Bamboo shrimps and African Filter Shrimps are filter feeders that take suspended plant and animal material. They will scavenge too, but prefer to be fed proprietary invertebrate filter feeds or ground fish flakes. Tropical and temperate (Amano, Cherry and Crystal Shrimp). Good water quality essential. Generally quite peaceful – most species can be kept, and do best in, groups. Many fish such as cichlids, loaches and pufferfish, will predate shrimps.

Some species have a larval planktonic stage that often requires a marine stage (such as Amano Shrimps) whilst others, such as Crystal Red Shrimps, do not.

Shrimps, like all invertebrates, are sensitive to copper-based fish medications. The Crystal Red Shrimp is a 'hobby shrimp' and is available in quality grades, with SSS considered the best. Shrimps moult their exoskeletons regularly as they grow – these may be seen occasionally and mistaken for dead shrimps.

Australian Redclaw Crayfish or Blue Lobster

Cherax quadricarinatus

Origin: Australia

Length: Males 20 to 25 cm (8 to 10 in)
females 18 cm (7 in)

Lifespan: 3 to 12 years

Adult males are larger and the outer pincer of the large claws is red. Omnivores. Will also predate on snails, shrimps and even fish if it can catch them, which it may do at night when the fish are sleeping. Tropical and temperate. Good water quality essential. Pairs can be kept, although females are territorial. Only keep with larger, robust fish. Egg-layer. This is the only legal aquarium crayfish in the UK as it needs temperatures above 10°C to survive. It has become a pest species in other parts of the world including Mexico and Jamaica. Sensitive to copper-based fish medications.

Weights & measures

If you prefer your units in pounds and inches, you can use this conversion chart:

Length in inches	Length in cm	Weight in kg	Weight in lbs
1	2.5	0.5	1.1
2	5.1	0.7	1.5
3	7.6	1	2.2
4	10.2	1.5	3.3
5	12.7	2	4.4
8	20.3	3	6.6
10	25.4	4	8.8
15	38.1	5	11

Measurements rounded to 1 decimal place.